D1882338

THE
CYCLE OF SPRING

Owing to the antiquity and rarity of this book, certain pages are regrettably absent, and readability is compromised due to the blurring of the original text. If you possess any insights regarding the availability of these missing sections, kindly inform us. Your assistance is crucial in ensuring the completion of this significant work for the benefit of future generations.

THE CYCLE OF SPRING

RABINDRANATH TAGORE

GYAN

Published by

Gyan Publishing House
5, Ansari Road
Daryaganj, New Delhi-110002
Phone: 011-47034999, 9811692060
E-mail: books@gyanbooks.com

Distribution Network
gyanbooks.com
India, USA, Canada, UK, Australia

© Publisher
All rights reserved. No part of this work may be reproduced, stored, adapted, or transmitted in any form or by any means, electronic, mechanical, photocopying, micro-filming, recording or otherwise, or translated in any language, without the prior written permission of the copyright owner and the publisher.

ISBN: 978-93-6780-397-4 (HB)

First Published, 1917

2nd Impression 2025

Printed at: Gyan Press, Delhi.

The book is sold subject to the condition that it shall not, by way of trade or otherwise, be lent, resold, hired out, or otherwise circulated without the prior publisher's written consent.

THE CYCLE OF SPRING
Author: SIR RABINDRANATH TAGORE

THE CYCLE OF SPRING

THE CYCLE OF SPRING

BY

SIR RABINDRANATH TAGORE

MACMILLAN AND CO., LIMITED
ST. MARTIN'S STREET, LONDON
1919

I DEDICATE THIS BOOK

TO MY BOYS OF THE SHANTINIKETAN

WHO HAVE FREED

THE FOUNTAIN OF YOUTH

HIDDEN IN THE HEART OF THIS OLD POET

AND TO DINENDRANATH

WHO IS

THE GUIDE OF THESE BOYS IN THEIR FESTIVALS

AND TREASURE-HOUSE OF ALL MY SONGS

The greater part of the introductory portion of this drama was translated from the original Bengali by Mr. C. F. Andrews and Prof. Nishikanta Sen, and revised by the Author.

INTRODUCTION

Characters of the Prelude

KING, VIZIER, GENERAL (BIJOY VARMA)

CHINESE AMBASSADOR, PUNDIT (SRUTI-BHUSHAN)

POET (KABI-SHEKHAR), GUARDS, COURTIERS, HERALD

The stage is on two levels: the higher, at the back, for the Song-preludes alone, concealed by a purple curtain; the lower only being discovered when the drop goes up. Diagonally across the extreme left of the lower stage, is arranged the king's court, with various platforms, for the various dignitaries ascending to the canopied throne.

The body of the stage is left free for the "Play" when that develops.

(*Enter some* COURTIERS.)

[The names of the speakers are not given in the margin, as they can easily be guessed.]

Hush! Hush!

What is the matter?

The King is in great distress.

How dreadful!

Who is that over there, playing on his flute?

Why? What's the matter?

The King is greatly disturbed.

How dreadful!

What are those wild children doing, making so much noise?

They are the Mandal family.

Then tell the Mandal family to keep their children quiet.

Where can that Vizier have gone to?

Here I am. What's the matter?

Haven't you heard the news?

No, what?

The King is greatly troubled in his mind.

Well, I've got some very important news about the frontier war.

War we may have, but not the news.

Then the Chinese Ambassador is waiting to see His Majesty.

Let him wait. Anyhow he can't see the King.

Can't see the King?—Ah, here is the King at last. Look at him coming this way, with a mirror in his hand. "Long live the King. Long live the King."

If it please Your Majesty, it is time to go to the Court.

Time to go ? Yes, time to go, but not to the Court.

What does Your Majesty mean ?

Haven't you heard ? The bell has just been rung to dismiss the Court.

When ? What bell ? We haven't heard any bell.

How could you hear ? They have rung it in my ears alone.

Oh, Sire. No one can have had the impertinence to do that.

Vizier ! They are ringing it now.

Pardon me, Sire, if I am very stupid ; but I cannot understand.

Look at this, Vizier, look at this.

Your Majesty's hair——

Can't you see there's a bell-ringer there ?

Oh, Your Majesty. Are you playing a joke?

The joke is not mine, but His, who has got the whole world by the ear, and is having His jest. Last night, when the Queen was putting a garland of jasmines round my neck, she cried out with alarm, "King, what is this? Here are two grey hairs behind your ear."

Oh, please, Sire, don't worry so much about a little thing like that. Why! The royal physician——

Vizier! The founder of our dynasty had his royal physician, too. But what could he do? Death has left his card of invitation behind my ear. The Queen wanted, then and there, to pluck out the grey hairs. But I said, "Queen, what's the use? You may remove Death's invitation, but

can you remove Death, the Inviter ?"
So, for the present——

Yes, Sire, for the present, let us attend to business.

Business, Vizier! I have no time for business. Send for the Pundit. Send for Sruti-bhushan.

But, Sire, the General——

The General?—No, no, not the General. Send for the Pundit.

But, the news from the frontier——

Vizier, the news has come to me from the last great frontier of all, the frontier of Death. Send for the Pundit.

But if Your Majesty will give me one moment, the Ambassador from the great Emperor of China——

Vizier, a greater Emperor has sent his embassy to me. Call Sruti-bhushan.

Very well, Sire. But your father-in-law——

It is not my father-in-law whom I want now. Send for the Pundit.

But, if it please you to hear me this once. The poet, Kabi-shekhar, is waiting with his new book called the *Garden of Poesy*.

Let your poet disport himself, jumping about on the topmost branches of his Garden of Poesy, but send for the Pundit.

Very well, Sire. I will send for him at once.

Tell him to bring his book of devotions with him, called the *Ocean of Renunciation*.

Yes, Sire.

But, Vizier. Who are those outside making all that noise? Go out and stop them at once. I must have peace.

If it please Your Majesty, there is a famine in Nagapatam and the headmen of the villages are praying to be allowed to see your face.

My time is short, Vizier. I must have peace.

They say their time is shorter. They are at death's door. They, too, want peace,—peace from the burning of hunger.

Vizier! The burning of hunger is quenched at last on the funeral pyre.

Then these wretched people——

Wretched!—Listen to the advice of a wretched King to his wretched subjects. It is futile to be impatient, and try to break through the net of the inexorable Fisherman. Sooner or later, Death the Fisherman will have his haul.

Well then?

Let me have the Pundit, and his *Book of Renunciation.*

And in this scarcity——

Vizier! The real scarcity is of time, and not of food. We are all suffering from starvation of time. None of us has enough of it, neither the King, nor his people.

Then——

Then know, that our petitions for more time will all go to the last fire of doom. So why strain our voice in prayer?—Ah, here is Sruti-bhushan at last. My reverence to you.

Pundit, do tell the King that the Goddess of Fortune deserts him who gives way to melancholy.

Sruti-bhushan, what is my Vizier whispering to you?

He tells me, King, to instruct you in the ways of fortune.

What instruction can you give ?

There is a verse in my book of devotions which runs as follows :

Fortune, as fickle as lotus-flower,
Closes her favours when comes the hour.
Oh, foolish man, how can you trust her,
Who comes of a sudden, and goes in a fluster ?

Ah, Pundit. One breath of your teaching blows out the false flame of ambition. Our teacher has said :

" Teeth fall out, hair grows grey,
Yet man clings to hope that plays him false."

Well, King, now that you have introduced the subject of hope, let me give you another verse from the *Ocean of Renunciation*. It runs as follows :

That fetters are binding, all are aware ;
But fetters of hope are strange, I declare.
Hope's captive is tossed in the whirlpool's wake,
And only grows still when the fetters break.

Ah, Pundit. Your words are priceless. Vizier, give him a hundred gold sequins at once. What's that noise outside ?

It is the famine-stricken people.

Tell them to hold their peace.

Let Sruti-bhushan, with his book of devotions, go and try to bring them peace ; and, in the meanwhile, Your Majesty might discuss war matters——

No, no. Let the war matters come later. I can't let Sruti-bhushan go yet.

King, you said something to me, a moment ago, about a gift of gold.

Now mere gold, by itself, does not confer any permanent benefit. It is said in my book of devotions, called the *Ocean of Renunciation*:

He who gives gold, gives only pain;
When the gold is spent grief comes again.
When a lakh, or crore, of gold is spent,
Grief only remains in the empty tent.

Ah, Pundit. How exquisite. So you don't want any gold, my Master?

No, King, I don't want gold, but something more permanent, which would make your merit permanent also. I should be quite content, if you gave me the living of Kanchanpur. For it is said in the *Renunciation*——

No, Pundit, I quite understand. You needn't quote scripture to support your claim. I understand quite well— Vizier!

Yes, Your Majesty.

See that the rich province of Kanchanpur is settled on the Pundit. —What's the matter now outside there? What are they crying for?

If it please Your Majesty, it is the people.

Why do they cry so repeatedly?

Their cry is repeated, I admit, but the reason remains most monotonously the same. They are starving.

But, King, I must tell you before I forget it. It is the one desire of my wife to make her whole body jingle, from head to foot, in praise of your munificence; but, alas, the sound is too feeble for want of proper ornaments.

I understand you, Pundit. Vizier! Order ornaments from the Court Jeweller for Sruti-bhushan's wife immediately.

And, King, while he is about it, would you tell the Vizier, that we are both of us distracted in our devotions by house-repairs. Let him ask the royal masons to put up a thoroughly well-built house, where we can practise our devotions in peace.

Very well, Pundit.— Vizier !

Yes, Your Majesty.

Give the order at once.

Sire, your treasury is empty. Funds are wanting.

Pooh ! That's an old story. I hear that every year. It is your business to increase the funds, and mine to increase the wants. What do you say, Sruti-bhushan ?

King, I cannot blame the Vizier. He is looking after your treasures in this world. We are looking after your treasures in the next. So where he sees want, we see wealth. Now, if you would only let me dive deep once more into the *Ocean of Renunciation* you will find it written as follows :

That King's coffers are well stored,
Where wealth alone on worth is poured.

Pundit, your company is most valuable.

Your Majesty, Sruti-bhushan knows its value to a farthing. Come, Sruti-bhushan, make haste. Let us collect all the wealth you need for your Treasury of Devotion. For wealth has the ugly habit of diminishing fast. If we are not quick about it, little will remain to enable us to observe our renunciation with all splendour.

Yes, Vizier, let us go at once. (*To the King.*) When he is making such a fuss about a tiny matter like this, it is best to pacify him first and then return to you afterwards.

Pundit, I am afraid that, some day, you will leave my royal protection altogether, and retire to the forest.

King, so long as I find contentment in a King's palace, it is as good as a hermitage for my peace of mind. I must now leave you, King. Vizier, let us go.

[*The Vizier and Pundit go out.*

Oh, dear me! Whatever shall I do? Here's the Poet coming. I am afraid he'll make me break all my good resolutions.—Oh, my grey hairs, cover my ears, so that the Poet's allurements may not enter.

Why, King, what's the matter? I hear you want to send away your Poet.

What have I to do with poets, when poetry brings me this parting message?

What parting message?

Look at this behind my ear. Don't you see it?

See what? Grey hairs? Why, King, don't you worry about that.

Poet, Nature is trying to rub out the green of youth, and to paint everything white.

No, no, King. You haven't understood the artist. On that white ground, Nature will paint new colours.

I don't see any sign of colours yet.

They are all within. In the heart of the white dwell all the colours of the rainbow.

Oh, Poet, do be quiet. You disturb me when you talk like that.

King, if this youth fades, let it fade. Another Queen of Youth is coming. And she is putting a garland of pure white jasmines round your head, in order to be your bride. The wedding festival is being made ready, behind the scene.

Oh, dear, Poet. You will undo everything. Do go away. Ho there, Guard. Go at once and call Srutibhushan.

What will you do with him, King, when he comes?

I will compose my mind, and practise my renunciation.

Ah, King, when I heard that news, I came at once. For I can be your companion in this practice of renunciation.

You?

Yes, I, King. We Poets exist for this very purpose. We set men free from their desires.

I don't understand you. You talk in riddles.

What? You don't understand me?

And yet you have been reading my poems all this while!—There is renunciation in our words, renunciation in the metre, renunciation in our music. That is why fortune always forsakes us; and we, in turn always forsake fortune. We go about, all day long, initiating the youths in the sacred cult of fortune-forsaking.

What does it say to us?

It says:

"Ah, brothers, don't cling to your goods and chattels,
And sit ever in the corner of your room.
Come out, come out into the open world.
Come out into the highways of life.
Come out, ye youthful Renouncers."

But, Poet, do you really mean to say that the highway of the open world is the pathway of renunciation?

Why not, King? In the open world all is change, all is life, all is movement. And he who ever moves and journeys with this life-movement, dancing and playing on his flute as he goes, he is the true Renouncer. He is the true disciple of the minstrel Poet.

But how then can I get peace? I must have peace.

Oh, King, we haven't the least desire for peace. We are the Renouncers.

But ought we not to get that treasure, which is said to be never-changing?

No, we don't covet any never-changing treasures. We are the Renouncers.

What do you mean? Oh, dear, Poet, you will undo everything, if you talk like that. You are destroying my peace of mind. Call Sruti-bhushan. Let some one call the Pundit.

What I mean, King, is this. We are the true Renouncers, because change is our very secret. We lose, in order to find. We have no faith in the never-changing.

What do you mean ?

Haven't you noticed the detachment of the rushing river, as it runs splashing from its mountain cave ? It gives itself away so swiftly, and only thus it finds itself. What is never-changing, for the river, is the desert sand, where it loses its course.

Ah, but listen, Poet—listen to those cries there outside. That is your world. How do you deal with that ?

King, they are your starving people.

My people, Poet ? Why do you call them that ? They are the world's people, not mine. Have I created their miseries? What can your youthful Poet Renouncers do to relieve sufferings like theirs? Tell me that.

King, it is we alone who can truly bear those sufferings, because we are like the river that flows on in gladness, thus lightening our burden, and the burden of the world. But the hard, metalled road is fixed and never-changing. And so it makes the burden more burdensome. The heavy loads groan and creak along it, and cut deep gashes in its breast. We Poets call to every one to carry all their joys and sorrows lightly, in a rhythmic measure. Our call is the Renouncers' call.

Ah, Poet, now I don't care a straw for Sruti-bhushan. Let the Pundit go hang. But, do you know what my trouble is now? Though I can't, for the life of me, understand your words, the music haunts me. Now, it's just the other way round with the Pundit. His words are clear enough, and they obey the rules of syntax quite correctly. But the tune!— No, it's no use telling you any further.

King, our words don't speak, they sing.

Well, Poet, what do you want to do now ?

King, I'm going to have a race through those cries, which are rising outside your gate.

What do you mean ? Famine relief is for men of business. Poets oughtn't to have anything to do with things like that.

King, business men always make their business so out of tune. That is why we Poets hasten to tune it.

Now come, my dear Poet, do speak in plainer language.

King, they work, because they must. We work, because we are in love with life. That is why they condemn us as unpractical, and we condemn them as lifeless.

But who is right, Poet? Who wins? You, or they?

We, King, we. We always win.

But, Poet, your proof——

King, the greatest things in the world disdain proof. But if you could for a time wipe out all the poets and all their poetry from the world, then you would soon discover, by their very absence, where the men of action got their energy from, and who really supplied the life-sap to their harvest-field. It is not those who have plunged deep down into the Pundit's *Ocean of Renunciation*, nor those who are always clinging to their possessions; it is not those who have become adepts in turning out quantities of work, nor those who are ever telling the dry beads of duty,—it is not these who win at last. But it is those who love, because they live. These truly win, for they truly surrender. They accept pain with all their strength and with all their strength they remove pain. It is they who create, because they know the secret of true joy, which is the secret of detachment.

Well then, Poet, if that be so, what do you ask me to do now ?

I ask you, King, to rise up and move. That cry outside yonder is the cry of life to life. And if the life within you is not stirred, in response to that call without, then there is cause for anxiety indeed,—not because duty has been neglected, but because you are dying.

But, Poet, surely we must die, sooner or later?

No, King, that's a lie. When we feel for certain that we are alive, then we know for certain that we shall go on living. Those who have never put life to the test, in all possible ways, these keep on crying out:

Life is fleeting, Life is waning,
Life is like a dew-drop on a lotus leaf.

But, isn't life inconstant?

Only because its movement is unceasing. The moment you stop this movement, that moment you begin to play the drama of Death.

Poet, are you speaking the truth? Shall we really go on living?

Yes, we shall really go on living.

Then, Poet, if we are going to go on living, we must make our life worth its eternity. Is not that so?

Yes, indeed.

Ho, Guard.

Yes, Your Royal Highness.

Call the Vizier at once.

Yes, Your Royal Highness.

(*Vizier enters.*)

What is Your Majesty's pleasure ?

Vizier ! Why on earth have you kept me waiting so long ?

I was very busy, Your Majesty.

Busy ? What were you busy about ?

I was dismissing the General.

Why should you dismiss the General ? We have got to discuss war matters with him.

And arrangements had to be made for the state-departure of the Chinese Ambassador.

What do you mean by his state-departure ?

If it please Your Majesty, you did not grant him an interview. So he——

Vizier! You surprise me. Is this the way you manage state affairs? What has happened to you? Have you lost your senses?

Then, again, Sire, I was trying to find a way to pull down the Poet's house. At first, no one would undertake it. Then, at last, all the Pundits of the Royal School of Grammar and Logic came up with their proper tools and set to work.

Vizier! Are you mad this morning? Pull down the Poet's house? Why, you might as well kill all the birds in the garden and make them up into a pie.

If it please Your Majesty, you need not be annoyed. We shan't have to pull down the house after all; for the moment Sruti-bhushan heard it was to be demolished, he decided to take possession of it himself.

What, Vizier! That's worse still. Why! The Goddess of Music would break her harp in pieces against my head, if she even heard of such a thing. No, that can't be.

Then, Your Majesty, there was another thing to be got through. We had to deliver over the province of Kanchanpur to the Pundit.

No, Vizier! What a mess you are making. That must go to our Poet.

To me, King? No. My poetry never accepts reward.

Well, well. Let the Pundit have it.

And, last of all, Sire. I have issued orders to the soldiers to disperse the crowd of famine-stricken people.

Vizier, you are doing nothing but

blunder. The best way to disperse the famished people is with food, not force.

(*Guard enters.*)

May it please Your Royal Highness.

What's the matter, Guard ?

May it please Your Royal Highness, here is Sruti-bhushan, the Pundit, coming back with his *Book of Devotions*.

Oh, stop him, Vizier, stop him. He will undo everything. Don't let him come upon me unawares like this. In a moment of weakness, I may suddenly find myself out of my depths in the *Ocean of Renunciation*. Poet ! Don't give me time for that. Do something. Do anything. Have you got anything ready to hand ? Any play toward ? Any poem ? Any masque ? Any——

Yes, King. I have got the very

thing. But whether it is a drama, or a poem, or a play, or a masque, I cannot say.

Shall I be able to understand the sense of what you have written?

No, King, what a poet writes is not meant to have any sense.

What then?

To have the tune itself.

What do you mean? Is there no philosophy in it?

No, none at all, thank goodness.

What does it say, then?

King, it says "I exist." Don't you know the meaning of the first cry of the new-born child? The child, when it is born, hears at once the cries of the earth and water and sky, which surround him,—and they all cry to him, "We exist," and his tiny little heart responds, and cries out in its turn, "I exist." My poetry is like the cry of that new-born child. It is a response to the cry of the Universe.

Is it nothing more than that, Poet?

No, nothing more. There is life in my song, which cries, "In joy and in sorrow, in work and in rest, in life and in death, in victory and in defeat, in this world and in the next, all hail to the 'I exist.'"

Well, Poet, I can assure you, if your play hasn't got any philosophy in it, it won't pass muster in these days.

That's true, King. The newer people, of this modern age, are more eager to amass than to realize. They are, in their generation, wiser than the children of light.

Whom shall we ask, then, for an audience? Shall we ask the young students of our royal school?

No, King, they cut up poetry with their logic. They are like the young-horned deer trying their new horns on the flower-beds.

Whom should I ask, then?

Ask those whose hair is turning grey.

What do you mean, Poet?

The youth of these middle-aged people is a youth of detachment. They have just crossed the waters of pleasure, and are in sight of the land of pure gladness. They don't want to eat fruit; but to produce it.

I, at least, have now reached that age of discretion, and ought to be able to appreciate your songs. Shall I ask the General?

Yes, ask him.

And the Chinese Ambassador?

Yes, ask him too.

I hear my father-in-law has come.

Well, ask him too, but I have my doubts about his youthful sons.

But don't forget his daughter.

Don't worry about her. She won't let herself be forgotten.

And Sruti-bhushan? Shall I ask him?

No, King, no. Decidedly, no. I have no grudge against him. Why should I inflict this on him?

Very well, Poet. Off with you. Make your stage preparations.

No, King. We are going to act this play without any special preparations. Truth looks tawdry when she is overdressed.

But, Poet, there must be some canvas for a background.

No. Our only background is the mind. On that we shall summon up a picture with the magic wand of music.

Are there any songs in the play?

Yes, King. The door of each act will be opened by the key of song.

What is the subject of the songs?

The Disrobing of Winter.

But, Poet, we haven't read about that in any Mythology.

In the world-myth this song comes round in its turn. In the play of the seasons, each year, the mask of the Old Man, Winter, is pulled off, and the form of Spring is revealed in all its beauty. Thus we see that the old is ever new.

Well, Poet, so much for the songs: but what about the remainder?

Oh, that is all about life.

Life? What is life?

This is how it runs: A band of

young companions has run off in pursuit of one Old Man. They have taken a vow to catch him. They enter into a cave; they take hold of him, and then——

Then, what? What did they see?

Ah. That will be told in its own good time.

But, I haven't understood one thing. Your drama and your songs,—have they different subjects, or the same?

The same, King. The play of Spring in nature is the counterpart of the play of Youth in our lives. It is simply from the lyrical drama of the World Poet that I have stolen this plot.

Who, then, are the chief characters?

One is called the Leader.

Who is he, Poet?

He is the guiding impulse in our life. Another is Chandra.

Who is he?

He who makes life dear to us.

And who else?

Then there is Dada, to whom duty is the essence of life, not joy.

Is there any one else?

Yes, the blind Minstrel.

Blind?

Because he does not see with his eyes, therefore he sees with his whole body and mind and soul.

Who else is there, in your play, among the chief actors?

You are there, King.

I?

Yes, you, King. For if you stayed out of it, instead of coming into it, then the King would begin to abuse the Poet and send for Sruti-bhushan again. And then there would be no hope of salvation for him. For the World Poet himself would be defeated. And the South Wind of Spring would have 'to retire, without receiving its homage.

ACT I

The Heralds of Spring are abroad. There are songs in the rustling bamboo leaves, in birds' nests, and in blossoming branches.

SONG-PRELUDE

The purple secondary curtain[1] *goes up, disclosing the elevated rear stage with a skyey background of dark blue, on which appear the horn of the crescent moon and the silver points of stars. Trees in the foreground, with two rope swings entwined with garlands of flowers. Flowers every-*

[1] Neither the secondary curtain nor the drop is again used during the play. The action is continuous, either on the front stage, or on the rear stage, the latter being darkened when not actually in use.

where in profusion. On the extreme left the mouth of a dark cavern dimly seen. Boys representing the " Bamboo " disclosed, swinging.

Song of the Bamboo

O South Wind, the Wanderer, come and rock me,
Rouse me into the rapture of new leaves.
I am the wayside bamboo tree, waiting for your breath
To tingle life into my branches.

O South Wind, the Wanderer, my dwelling is in the end of the lane.
I know your wayfaring, and the language of your footsteps.
Your least touch thrills me out of my slumber,
Your whisper gleans my secrets.

(Enter a troop of girls, dancing, representing birds.)

Song of the Bird

The sky pours its light into our hearts,
We fill the sky with songs in answer.
We pelt the air with our notes
When the air stirs our wings with its madness.
O Flame of the Forest,
All your flower-torches are ablaze;
You have kissed our songs red with the passion of your youth.
In the spring breeze the mango-blossoms launch their messages to the unknown
And the new leaves dream aloud all day.
O Sirish, you have cast your perfume-net round our hearts,
Drawing them out in songs.

(*Disclosed among the branches of trees, suddenly lighted up, boys representing champak blossoms.*)

Song of the Blossoming Champak

My shadow dances in your waves,
everflowing river,
I, the blossoming champak, stand unmoved on the bank,
with my flower-vigils.
My movement dwells in the stillness of my depth,
In the delicious birth of new leaves,
In flood of flowers,
In unseen urge of new life towards the light.
Its stirring thrills the sky, and the silence of the dawn is moved.

Morning

[*The rear stage is now darkened. On the main stage, bright, enter a band of youths whose number may be anything between three and thirty. They sing.*]

The fire of April leaps from forest to forest,
Flashing up in leaves and flowers
from all nooks and corners.
The sky is thriftless with colours,
The air delirious with songs.
The wind-tost branches of the woodland
Spread their unrest in our blood.
The air is filled with bewilderment of mirth ;
And the breeze rushes from flower to flower, asking their names.

[In the following dialogue only the names of the principal characters are given. Wherever the name is not given the speaker is one or other of the Youths.]

April pulls hard, brother, April pulls very hard.

How do you know that ?

If he didn't, he would never have pulled Dada outside his den.

Well, I declare. Here is Dada, our cargo-boat of moral-maxims, towed against the current of his own pen and ink.

Chandra

But you mustn't give April all the credit for that. For I, Chandra, have hidden the yellow leaves of his manuscript book among the young buds of the *pial* forest, and Dada is out looking for it.

The manuscript book banished! What a good riddance!

We ought to strip off Dada's grey philosopher's cloak also.

Chandra

Yes, the very dust of the earth is tingling with youth, and yet there's not a single touch of Spring in the whole of Dada's body.

Dada

Oh, do stop this fooling. What a nuisance you are making of yourselves! We aren't children any longer.

Chandra

Dada, the age of this earth is scarcely less than yours; and yet it is not ashamed to look fresh.

Dada, you are always struggling with those quatrains of yours, full of advice that is as old as death, while the earth and the water are ever striving to be new.

Dada, how in the world can you go on writing verses like that, sitting in your den?

Dada

Well, you see, I don't cultivate poetry, as an amateur gardener cultivates flowers. *My* poems have substance and weight in them.

Yes, they are like the turnips, which cling to the ground.

Dada

Well, then, listen to me——

How awful! Here's Dada going to run amuck with his quatrains.

Oh dear, oh dear! The quatrains are let loose. There's no holding them in.

To all passers-by I give notice that Dada's quatrains have gone mad, and are running amuck.

Chandra

Dada! Don't take any notice of their fun. Go on with your reading. If no one else can survive it, I think I can. I am not a coward like these fellows.

Come on, then, Dada. We won't

be cowards. We will keep our ground, and not yield an inch, but only listen.

We will receive the spear-thrusts of the quatrains on our breast, not on our back.

But for pity's sake, Dada, give us only one—not more.

Dada

Very well. Now listen :

If bamboos were made only into flutes,
They would droop and die with very
shame,
They hold their heads high in the sky,
Because they are variously useful.

Please, gentlemen, don't laugh. Have patience while I explain. The meaning is——

The meaning ?

What ? Must the infantry charge of meaning follow the cannonading of your quatrains, to complete the rout?

Dada

Just one word to make you understand. It means, that if the bamboos were no better than those noisy instruments——

No, Dada, we must not understand.

I defy you to make us understand.

Dada, if you use force to make us understand we shall use force to force ourselves not to understand.

Dada

The gist of the quatrain is this, that if we do no good to the world, then——

Then the world will be very greatly relieved.

Dada

There is another verse that makes it clearer:

There are numerous stars in the mid-
night sky,
Which hang in the air for no purpose;
If they would only come down to earth,
For the street lighting they might be
useful.

I see we must make clearer our meaning. Catch him. Let's raise him up, shoulder high, and take him back to his den.

Dada

Why are you so excited to-day? Have you any particular business to do?

Yes, we have very urgent business, —very urgent indeed.

Dada

What is your business about?

We are out to seek a play for our Spring festival.

Dada

Play! Day and night, play!

(*They sing.*)

We are free, my friends, from the fear of work,
For we know that work is play,—
the play of life.
It is Play, to fight and toss,
between life and death;
It is Play that flashes in the laughter of light in the infinite heart;
It roars in the wind,
and surges in the sea.

Oh, here comes our Leader. Brothers—our Leader, our Leader.

Leader

Hallo! What a noise you make!

Was it that which made you come out of doors?

Leader

Yes.

Well, we did it for that very purpose.

Leader

You don't want me to remain in-doors ?

Why remain indoors ? This outer world has been made with a lavish expenditure of sun and moon and stars. Let us enjoy it, and then we can save God's face for indulging in such extravagance.

Leader

What were you discussing ?

This :

(*They sing.*)

Play blooms in flower
and ripens in fruit
In the sunshine of eternal youth.
Play bursts up in the blood-red fire,
and licks into ashes the decaying
and the dead.

Our Dada's objection was about this play.

Dada

Shall I tell you the reason why?

Yes, Dada, you may tell us, but we shan't promise to listen.

Dada

Here it is:

Time is the capital of work,
And Play is its defalcation.
Play rifles the house, and then wastes its spoil,
Therefore the wise call it worse than useless.

Chandra

But surely, Dada, you are talking nonsense. Time itself is Play. Its only object is Pas-time.

Dada

Then what is Work?

Chandra

Work is the dust raised by the passing of Time.

Dada

Leader, you must give us your answers.

Leader

No. I never give answers. I lead on from one question to another. That is my leadership.

Dada

Everything else has its limits, but your childishness is absolutely unbounded.

Do you know the reason? It is because we are really nothing but children. And everything else has its limitations except the child.

Dada

Won't you ever attain Age?

No, we shall never attain Age.

We shall die old, but never attain Age.

Chandra

When we meet Age, we shall shave his head, and put him on a donkey, and send him across the river.

Oh, you can save yourself the trouble of shaving his head for Age is bald.

(They sing.)

Our hair shall never turn grey,
Never.
There is no blank in this world for us,
no break in our road,
It may be an illusion that we follow,
But it shall never play us false,
Never.

(The Leader sings.)

Our hair shall never turn grey,
Never.

We will never doubt the world and shut
our eyes to ponder.
Never.
We will not grope in the maze of our
mind.
We flow with the flood of things, from
the mountain to the sea,
We will never be lost in the desert sand,
Never.

We can tell, by his looks, that Dada will some day go to that Old Man, to receive his lessons.

Leader

Which Old Man ?

The Old Man of the line of Adam.

He dwells in a cave, and never thinks of dying.

Leader

Where did you learn about him ?

Oh, every one talks about him, And it is in the books also.

Leader

What does he look like?

Some say he is white, like the skull of a dead man. And some say he is dark, like the socket of a skeleton's eye.

But haven't you heard any news of him, Leader?

Leader

I don't believe in him at all.

Well, that goes entirely against current opinion. That Old Man is more existent than anything else. He lives within the ribs of creation.

According to our Pundit, it is we who have no existence. You can't be certain whether we are, or are not.

Chandra

We? Oh, we are too brand new

altogether. We haven't yet got our credentials to prove that we exist.

Leader

Have you really gone and opened communication with the Pundits ?

Why ? What harm is there in that, Leader ?

Leader

You will become pale, like the white mist in autumn. Even the least colour of blood will disappear from your mind. I have a suggestion.

What, Leader ? What ?

Leader

You were looking out for a play ?

Yes, yes, we got quite frantic about it.

We thought it over so vigorously, that people had to run to the King's court to lodge a complaint.

Leader

Well, I can suggest a play which will be new.

What?—What?—Tell us.

Leader

Go and capture the Old Man.

That is new, no doubt, but we very much doubt if it's a play.

Leader

I am sure you won't be able to do it.

Not do it? We shall.

Leader

No, never.

Well then, suppose we do capture him, what will you give us?

Leader

I shall accept you as my preceptor.

Preceptor! You want to make us

grey, and cold, and old, before our time.

Leader

Then, what do you want me to do?

If we capture him, then we shall take away your leadership.

Leader

That will be a great relief to me. You have made all my bones out of joint already. Very well, then it's all settled?

Yes, settled. We shall bring him to you by the next full moon of Spring.

But what are we going to do with him?

Leader

You shall let him join in your Spring Festival.

Oh no, that will be outrageous.

Then the mango flowers will run to seed at once.

And all the cuckoos will become owls.

And the bees will go about reciting Sanskrit verses, making the air hum with m's and n's.

Leader

And your skull will be so top-heavy with prudence, that it will be difficult for you to keep on your feet.

How awful!

Leader

And you will have rheumatics in all your joints.

How awful!

Leader

And you will become your own elder

brothers, pulling your own ears to set yourselves right.

How awful!

Leader

And——

No more "ands." We are ready to surrender.

We will abandon our game of capturing the Old Man.

We will put it off till the cold weather. In this Springtime, your company will be enough for us.

Leader

Ah, I see! You have already got the chill of the Old Man in your bones.

Why? What are the symptoms?

Leader

You have no enthusiasm. You

back out at the very start. Why don't you make a trial?

Very well. Agreed. Come on.

Let us go after the Old Man. We will pluck him out, like a grey hair, wherever we find him.

Leader

But the Old Man is an adept in the business of plucking out. His best weapon is the hoe.

You needn't try to frighten us like that. When we are out for adventure, we must leave behind all fears, all quatrains, all Pundits, and all Scriptures.

(*They sing.*)

We are out on our way
And we fear not the Robber, the Old Man.
Our path is straight, it is broad,

Our burden is light, for our pocket is bare,
Who can rob us of our folly?
For us there is no rest, nor ease, nor praise, nor success,
We dance in the measure of fortune's rise and fall,
We play our game, or win or lose,
And we fear not the Robber.

ACT II

SONG-PRELUDE

[*Spring's Heralds try to rob Winter of his outfit of age.*]

Rear stage lighted up, disclosing Old Winter teased by the boys and girls representing Spring's Heralds.

SONG OF THE HERALDS OF SPRING

We seek our playmates,
Waking them up from all corners
before it is morning.
We call them in bird songs,
Beckon them in nodding branches.
We spread our spell for them
in the splendour of clouds.

We laugh at solemn Death
Till he joins in our laughter.
We tear open Time's purse,
Taking back his plunder from him.
You shall lose your heart to us, O Winter.
It will gleam in the trembling leaves
And break into flowers.

SONG OF WINTER

Leave me, let me go.
I sail for the bleak North, for the peace of the frozen shore.
Your laughter is untimely, my friends.
You turn my farewell tunes into the welcome song of the Newcomer,
And all things draw me back again into the dancing ring of their hearts.

SONG OF THE HERALDS OF SPRING

Life's spies are we, lurking in ambush everywhere.

We wait to rob you of your last
savings of withered hours
to scatter them in the wayward
winds.
We shall bind you in flower chains
where Spring keeps his captives,
For we know you carry your jewels
of youth
hidden in your grey rags.

(*Noon*)

[*The rear stage is darkened. The band of Youths enters on the main stage. No actual change in the scenery is necessary — this being left to the imagination of the audience.*]

Ferryman! Ferryman! Open your door.

Ferryman

What do you want?

We want the Old Man.

Ferryman

Which old man ?

Not which old man. We want *the* Old Man.

Ferryman

Who is he ?

The true and original Old Man.

Ferryman

Oh ! I understand. What do you want him for ?

For our Spring Festival.

Ferryman

For your Spring Festival ? Are you become mad ?

Not a sudden becoming. We have been like this from the beginning.

And we shall go on like this to the end.

(*They sing.*)

The Piper pipes in the centre, hidden from sight,
And we become frantic, we dance.
The March wind, seized with frenzy,
Runs and reels, and sways with noisy branches.
The sun and stars are drawn in the whirl of rapture.

Now, Ferryman, give us news of the Old Man.

You ply your boat from one landing stage to another. Surely you know where——

Ferryman

My business is limited only to the path. But whose path it is, and what it means, I have no occasion to enquire. For my goal is the landing-stage, not the house.

Very well. Let us go, let us try all the ways.

(*They sing.*)

The Piper pipes in the centre, hidden from sight.
Ah, the turbulent tune, to whose time the oceans dance,
And dance our heaving hearts.
Fling away all burdens and cares, brother,
Do not be doubtful of your path,
For the path wakes up of itself
Under the dancing steps of freedom.

Ferryman

There comes the Watchman. Ask him. I know about the way; but he knows about the wayfarers.

Watchman

Who are you?

We are just what you see. That's our only description.

Watchman

But what do you want ?

We want the Old Man.

Watchman

Which old man ?

That eternal Old Man.

Watchman

How absurd ! While you are seeking him, he is after you.

Why ?

Watchman

He is fond of warming his cold blood with the wine of hot youth.

We'll give him a warm enough reception. All we want is to see him. Have you seen him ?

Watchman

My watch is at night. I see my

people, but don't know their features. But, look here, every one knows that he is the great kidnapper; and you want to kidnap him! It's midsummer madness.

The secret is out. It doesn't take long to discover that we are mad.

Watchman

I am the Watchman. The people I see passing along the road are all very much alike. Therefore, when I see anything queer, it always strikes me.

Just listen to him. All the respectable people of our neighbourhood say just the same thing—that we are queer.

Yes, we're queer. There's no mistake about that.

Watchman

But all this is utter childishness.

Do you hear that? It's exactly what our Dada says.

We have been going on with our childishness through unremembered ages.

And now we have become confirmed children.

And we have a leader, who is a perfect veteran in childhood. He rushes along so recklessly, that he drops off his age at every step he runs.

Watchman

And who are you?

We are butterflies, freed from the cocoon of Age.

Watchman

[*Aside.*] Mad. Raving mad.

Ferryman

Then what will you all do now?

Chandra

We shall go——

Watchman

Where ?

Chandra

That we haven't decided.

Watchman

You have decided to go, but not where to go ?

Chandra

Yes, that will be settled as we go along.

Watchman

What does that mean ?

Chandra

It means this song.

(*They sing.*)

We move and move without rest,

We move while the wanderers' stars shine in the sky and fade.
We play the tune of the road
While our limbs scatter away the laughter of movement,
And our many-coloured mantle of youth flutters about in the air.

Watchman

Is it your custom to answer questions by songs?

Chandra

Yes, otherwise the answer becomes too unintelligible.

Watchman

Then you think your songs intelligible?

Chandra

Yes, quite, because they contain music.

(*They sing.*)

We move and move without rest.
World, the Rover, loves his comrades of the road.
His call comes across the sky,
The seasons lead the way, strewing the path with flowers.

Watchman

No ordinary being ever breaks out singing, like this, in the middle of talking.

Chandra

Again we are found out. We are no ordinary beings.

Watchman

Have you got no work to do?

Chandra

No, we are on a holiday.

Watchman

Why ?

Chandra

Lest our time should all be wasted.

Watchman

I don't quite understand you.

Chandra

Then we shall be obliged to sing again.

Watchman

No, no. There's no need to do that. I don't hope to understand you any better, even if you do sing.

Chandra

Everybody has given up the hope of understanding us.

Watchman

But how can things get on with you, if you behave like this ?

Chandra

Oh, there's no need for things to get on with us, so long as we ourselves get on.

Watchman

Mad! Quite mad! Raving mad!

Chandra

Why, here comes our Dada.

Dada, what made you lag behind?

Chandra

Don't you know? We are free as the wind, because we have no substance in us. But Dada is like the rain-cloud of August. He must stop, every now and then, to unburden himself.

Dada

Who are you?

Ferryman

I am the Ferryman.

Dada

And who are you ?

Watchman

I am the Watchman.

Dada

I am delighted to see you. I want to read you something that I have written. It contains nothing frivolous, but only the most important lessons.

Ferryman

Very good. Let us have it then.

Watchman

Our master used to tell us that there are plenty of men to say good things, but very few to listen. That requires strength of mind. Now, go on, Sir, go on.

Dada

I saw, in the street, one of the King's officers dragging along a merchant. The King had made up a false charge, in order to get his money. This gave me an inspiration. You must know that I never write a single line which is not inspired by some actual fact. You can put my verses to the test in the open streets and markets——

Ferryman

Please, Sir, do let us hear what you have written.

Dada

The sugar-cane filling itself with juice
Is chewed and sucked dry by all beggars.
O foolish men, take your lesson from
this;
Those trees are saved, which are fruitful.

You will understand that the sugar-cane gets into trouble, simply because it tries to keep its juice. But nobody is so foolish as to kill the tree that freely gives fruit.

Watchman

What splendid writing, Ferryman!

Ferryman

Yes, Watchman, it contains great lessons for us.

Watchman

It gives me food for thought. If only I had here our neighbour, the Scribe! I should like to take this down. Do send round to tell the people of the place to assemble.

Chandra

But, Ferryman, you promised to come out with us. Yet, if once Dada begins to quote his quatrains, there will be——

Ferryman

Go along with you. None of your madness here. We are fortunate now in having met our master. Let us improve the occasion with good words. We are all of us getting old. Who knows when we shall die?

All the more reason why you should cultivate our company.

Chandra

You can always find another Dada. But when once we are dead, God will never repeat the blunder of another absurdity like us again.

(*Enter Oilman.*)

Oilman

Ho! Watchman.

Watchman

Who is there? Is that the Oilman?

Oilman

The child I was bringing up was kidnapped last night.

Watchman

By whom?

Oilman

By the Old Man.

Youths

[*Together.*] Old Man? You don't mean it. Old Man?

Oilman

Yes, Sirs, the Old Man; what makes you so glad?

Oh, that's a bad habit of ours. We become glad for no reason whatever.

Watchman

[*Aside.*] Mad! Raving mad!

Have you seen the Old Man?

Oilman

I think I saw him in the distance last night.

First Youth

What did he look like?

Oilman

Black. More black than our brother here, the Watchman. Black as night, with two eyes on his breast shining like two glow-worms.

That won't suit us. That would be awkward for our Spring Festival.

Chandra

We shall have to change our date from the full moon to the dark moon.

For the dark moon has no end of eyes on her breast.

Watchman

But I warn you, my friends, you are not doing wisely.

No, we are not.

We are found out again. We never do anything wisely. It is contrary to our habit.

Watchman

Do you take this to be a joke? I warn you, my friends, it is dangerous.

Dangerous? That's the best joke of all.

(*They sing.*)

We are neither too good nor wise,
That is all the merit we have.
Our calumny spreads from land to land,
And danger dogs our steps.
We take great care to forget what is taught us,

We say things different from the book,
Bringing upon us trouble,
And rebuke from the learned.

Watchman

Ah, Sir, you spoke about some Leader. Where is he? He could have kept you in order, if he were with you.

He never stays with us, lest he should have to keep us in order.

He simply launches us on our way, and then slips off.

Watchman

That's a poor idea of leadership.

Chandra

He is never concerned about his leadership. That is why we recognize him as our Leader.

Watchman

Then he has got a very easy task.

Chandra

It is no easy task to lead men. But it is easy enough to drive them.

(They sing.)

We are not too good nor wise,
That is all the merit we have.
In a luckless moment we were born,
When the star of wisdom was the dimmest.
We can hope for no profit from our adventures,
We move on, because we must.

Dada, come on. Let us go.

Watchman

No, no, Sir. Don't you get yourself into mischief in their company.

Ferryman

You read your verses, Sir, to us. Our neighbours will be here soon. They will be greatly profited.

Dada

No. I'm not going to move a step from here.

Then let us move. The men in the street can't bear us.

That's because we rattle them too much.

You hear the hum of human bees, they smell the honey of Dada's quatrains.

Youths

[*Together.*] They come! They come!

(*Enter Village folk.*)

Villager

Is it true that there is going to be a reading?

Who are you? Are *you* going to read?

No. We commit all kinds of atrocities, but not that. This one merit will bring us salvation.

Villager

What do they say? They seem to be talking in riddles.

Chandra

We only say things which we perfectly understand ourselves, and they are riddles to you. Dada repeats to you things which you understand perfectly and these sound to you the very essence of wisdom.

(*Boy enters.*)

Boy

I couldn't catch him.

Whom?

Boy

The Old Man, whom you are seeking.

Have you seen him?

Boy

Yes, I thought I saw him going by in a car.

Where ? In what direction ?

Boy

I couldn't make out exactly. The dust raised by his wheels is still whirling in the air.

Then let us go.

He has filled the sky with dead leaves.

[*They go out.*

Watchman

They are mad ! Quite mad ! Raving mad !

ACT III

SONG-PRELUDE

[*Winter is being unmasked—his hidden youth about to be disclosed.*]

The rear stage lighted up, disclosing Winter and the Heralds of Spring.

Song of the Heralds of Spring

How grave he looks,
how laughably old,
How solemnly quiet among death preparations!
Come, friends, help him to find himself before he reaches home.
Change his pilgrim's robe
into the dress of the singing youth,

Snatch away his bag of dead things
And confound his calculations.

(*Another group sings.*)

The time comes when the world shall know
that you're not banished in your own shadows;
Your heart shall burst in torrents
Out of the clasp of the ice;
And your North wind turn its face
Against the haunts of the flitting phantoms.
There sounds the magician's drum,
And the sun waits with laughter in his glance,
To see your grey turn into green.

(*Evening*)

[*The rear stage is darkened; the light on the main stage dimmed to the greyness of dark.*]

Band of Youths

They all cry, "There, there," and when we look for it, we find nothing but dust and dry leaves.

I thought I had a glimpse of the flag on his car through the cloud.

It is difficult to follow his track. Now it seems East: now it seems West.

And so we are tired, chasing shadows all day long. And the day has been lost.

I tell you the truth. Fear comes more and more into my mind, as the day passes.

We have made a mistake. The morning light whispered in our ears, "Bravo, march on." And now, the evening light is mocking us for that.

I am afraid we have been deceived. I am beginning to feel greater respect for Dada's quatrains than before. We shall all be soon sitting down on the ground composing quatrains.

And then the whole neighbourhood will come, swarming round us. And they will get such immense benefit from our wisdom that they will never leave us.

And we shall settle down like a great big boulder, cold and immovable.

And they will cling to us, as we sit there, like a thick fog.

What would our Leader think of us, I wonder, if he could hear us now?

I am sure it is our Leader, who has led us astray. He makes us toil for nothing, while he himself remains idle.

Let us go back and fight with him. We will tell him that we won't move a step further, but sit with our legs tucked under us. These legs are wretched vagabonds. They are always trudging the road.

We will keep our hands fast behind our backs.

There is no mischief in the back ; all the trouble is in the front.

Of all our limbs, the back is the most truthful. It says to us, "Lie down."

When we are young, that braggart breast is a great swell ; but, in the end, we can only rely on our back.

The little stream that flows past our village comes to my mind. That morning we thought that it said to us, "Forward ! Forward !" But what it really said was, "False ! False !" The world is all false.

Our Pundit used to tell us that.

We shall go straight to the Pundit, when we get back.

We shall never stir one step outside the limit of the Pundit's Scriptures.

What a mistake we made. We thought that moving itself was something heroic.

But really not to move, that is heroic, because it is defying the whole moving world.

Brave rebels that we are, we shall *not* move. We shall have the audacity to sit still, and never move an inch.

"Life and youth are fleeting," the Scripture says. Let life and youth go to the dogs, we shall not move.

"Our minds and wealth are fleeting," adds the Scripture. "Give them up and sit still," say we.

Let us go back to the point from which we started.

But that would be to move.

What then?

There sit down, where we have come to.

And let us imagine that there we had been before we ever came there.

Yes, yes, that will keep our minds still. If we know that we have come from somewhere else, then the mind longs for that somewhere else.

That land of somewhere else is a very dangerous place.

There the ground moves, and also the roads. But as for us——

(*They sing.*)

We cling to our seats and never stir,
We allow our flowers to fade in peace,
and avoid the trouble of bearing
fruit.
Let the starlights blazon their eternal
folly,
We quench our flames.
Let the forest rustle and the ocean roar,

We sit mute.
Let the call of the flood-tide come from the sea,
We remain still.

Do you hear that laughter?

Yes, yes, it is laughter.

What a relief! We have never heard that sound for an age.

We had been choking, for want of the breath of laughter.

This laughter comes to us like the April rain.

Whose is it?

Cannot you guess? It is our Chandra.

What a marvellous gift of laughter he has! It is like a waterfall. It dashes all the black stones out of the path.

It is like sunlight. It cuts the mist to pieces with its sword.

Now all danger of quatrain fever is over. Let us get up.

From this moment there will be nothing but work for us. As the Scripture says, "Everything in this world is fleeting, and he only lives who does his duty and achieves fame."

Why are you quoting that? Are you still suffering from the quatrain fever?

What do you mean by fame? Does the river take any heed of its foam? Fame is that foam on life's stream.

(*Enter Chandra with a blind Minstrel.*)

Well, Chandra, what makes you so glad?

Chandra

I have got the track of the Old Man.

From whom?

Chandra

From this old Minstrel.

He seems to be blind.

Chandra

Yes, that is why he has not got to seek the road.

What do you say? Shall you be able to lead us right?

Minstrel

Yes.

But how?

Minstrel

Because I can hear the footsteps.

We also have ears, but——

Minstrel

I hear with my whole being.

Chandra

They all started up with fear, when I asked about the Old Man. Only this Minstrel seemed to have no fear. I suppose because he cannot see, he is not afraid.

Minstrel

Do you know why I have no fear? When the sun of my life set, and I became blind, the dark night revealed all its lights, and, from that day forward, I have been no more afraid of the dark.

Then let us go. The evening star is up.

Minstrel

Let me sing, and walk on as I sing, and you follow me. I cannot find my way, if I do not sing.

What do you mean?

Minstrel

My songs precede, I follow.

(*He sings.*)

Gently, my friend, gently walk to your
silent chamber.

I know not the way, I have not the light,
Dark is my life and my world.
I have only the sound of your steps
to guide me in this wilderness.

Gently, my friend, gently walk along the dark shore.
Let the hint of the way come in whisper,
Through the night, in the April breeze.
I have only the scent of your garland
to guide me in this wilderness.

ACT IV

SONG-PRELUDE

[*There enter a troupe of young things, and they introduce themselves in a song as follows :*]

THE SONG OF RETURNING YOUTH

Again and again we say " Good-bye,"
To come back again and again.
Oh, who are you?
I am the flower vakul.
And who are you?
I am the flower parul.
And who are these?
We are mango blossoms landed on the shore of light.

We laugh and take leave when the time beckons us.

We rush into the arms of the ever-returning.

But who are you?

I am the flower shimul.

And who are you?

I am the kamini *bunch,*

And who are these?

We are the jostling crowd of new leaves.

[*Winter is revealed as Spring and answers to the questions put by the chorus of young things.*]

The Song of Burdens dropped

Do you own defeat at the hand of youth?

Yes.

Have you met at last the ageless Old, who ever grows new?

Yes.

Have you come out of the walls that crumble and bury those whom they shelter?
Yes.

(*Another group sings.*)

Do you own defeat at the hands of life?
Yes.
Have you passed through death to stand at last face to face with the Deathless?
Yes.
Have you dealt the blow to the demon dust, that swallows your city Immortal?
Yes.

(*Spring's flowers surround him and sing.*)

THE SONG OF FRESH BEAUTY

We waited by the wayside counting moments
till you appeared in the April morning.

You come as a soldier-boy winning
life at death's gate,—
Oh, the wonder of it.
We listen amazed at the music of your
young voice.
Your mantle is blown in the wind
like the fragrance of the Spring.
The white spray of malati *flowers in*
your hair
shines like star-clusters.
A fire burns through the veil of your
smile,—
Oh, the wonder of it.
And who knows where your arrows
are hidden
which smite death?

(*Night*)

[*The rear stage is darkened, and the light on the main stage dimmed to the heavy purple blackness of mourning.*]

(*Enter the Band of Youths.*)

Chandra has gone away again, leaving us behind.

It is difficult to keep him still.

We get our rest by sitting down, but he gets his by walking on.

He has gone across the river with the blind minstrel, in whose depth of blindness Chandra is seeking the invisible light.

That is why our Leader calls him the Diver.

Our life becomes utterly empty, when Chandra is away.

Do you feel as though something was in the air ?

The sky seems to be looking into our face, like a friend bidding farewell.

This little stream of water is trickling through the *casuarina* grove. It seems like the tears of midnight.

We have never gazed upon the earth before with such intentness.

When we run forward at full speed, our eyes keep gazing in front of us, and we see nothing on either side of us.

If things did not move on and vanish, we should see no beauty anywhere.

If youth had only the heat of movement, it would get parched and withered. But there is ever the hidden tear, which keeps it fresh.

The cry of the world is not only "I have," but also "I give." In the first dawning light of creation, "I have" was wedded to "I give." If this bond of union were to snap, then everything would go to ruin.

I don't know where that blind Minstrel has landed us at last.

It seems as though these stars in

the sky above us are the gazing of countless eyes we met in all forgotten ages. It seems as if, through the flowers, there came the whisper of those we have forgotten, saying Remember us.

Our hearts will break if we do not sing.

(*They sing.*)

Did you leave behind you your love,
my heart,
and miss peace through all your
days?
And is the path you followed lost and
forgotten,
making your return hopeless?
I go roaming listening to brooks' babble,
to the rustle of leaves.
And it seems to me that I shall find the
way,
that reaches the land of lost love
beyond the evening stars.

What a strange tune is this, that comes out of the music of Spring.

It seems like the tune of yellow leaves.

Spring has stored up its tears in secret for us all this while.

It was afraid we should not understand it, because we were so youthful.

It wanted to beguile us with smiles.

But we shall sleep our hearts tonight in the sadness of the other shore.

Ah, the dear earth! The beautiful earth! She wants all that we have—the touch of our hands, the song of our hearts.

She wants to draw out from us all that is within, hidden even from ourselves.

This is her sorrow, that she finds out some things only to know that she has not found all. She loses before she attains.

Ah, the dear earth! We shall never deceive you.

(*They sing.*)

I shall crown you with my garland,
before I take leave.
You ever spoke to me in all my joys
and sorrows.
And now, at the end of the day, my
own heart will break in speech.
Words came to me, but not the tune,
and the song that I never sang
to you
remains hidden behind my tears.

Brother, did you notice that some one seemed to have passed by?

The only thing you feel is this passing by.

I felt the touch of the mantle of some wayfarer.

We came out to capture somebody, but now we feel the longing to be captured ourselves.

Ah, here comes the Minstrel. Where have you brought us ? The breath of the wayfaring world touches us here,—the breath of the starry sky.

We came seeking a new form of play. But now we have forgotten what play it was.

We wanted to catch the Old Man.

And everybody said that he was terrifying, a bodiless head, a gaping mouth, a dragon eager to swallow the moon of the youth of the world. But now we are no longer afraid. The flowers go, the leaves go, the waves in the river go, and we shall also follow them. Ah, blind Minstrel, strike your lute and sing to us. Who knows what is the hour of the night ?

(*The Minstrel sings.*)

Let me give my all to him, before I am asked,
whom the world offers its all.
When I came to him for my gifts, I was not afraid ;
And I will not fear, when I come to him,
to give up what I have.
The morning accepts his gold with songs,
the evening pays him back the debt of gold and is glad.
The joy of the blooming flower comes to fruit
with shedding of its leaves.
Hasten, my heart, and spend yourself in love,
before the day is done.

Minstrel, why is Chandra still absent ?

Minstrel

Don't you know that he has gone ?

Gone ?—Where ?

Minstrel

He said, I shall go and conquer him.

Whom ?

Minstrel

The One who is feared by all. He said, " Why else am I young ? "

Ah, that was fine.—Dada goes to read his quatrains to the village people, and Chandra has disappeared,—for what purpose nobody knows.

Minstrel

He said, " Men have always been fighting for a cause. It is the shock of that, which ruffles the breeze of this Spring."

The shock ?

Minstrel

Yes, the message that man's fight is not yet over.

Is this the message of Spring?

Minstrel

Yes. Those, who have been made immortal by death, have sent their message in these fresh leaves of Spring. It said, "We never doubted the way. We never counted the cost: we rushed out: we blossomed. If we had sat down to debate, then where would be the Spring?"

Has that made Chandra mad?

Minstrel

He said——

(*The Minstrel sings.*)

The Spring flowers have woven my wreath of victory,
The South wind breathes its breath of fire in my blood.
The voice of the house-corner wails in vain from behind.

Death stands before me, offering its crown.
The tempest of youth sweeps the sky-harp with its fingers;
My heart dances in its wild rhythm.
Gathering and storing are not for me,
I spend and scatter.
And prudence and comfort bid me adieu in despair.

But where has he gone to?

Minstrel

He said, "I cannot keep waiting by the wayside any longer. I must go and meet him, and conquer him."

But which way did he take?

Minstrel

He has entered the cave.

How is that? It is so fearfully dark. Did he, without making any enquiries——

Minstrel

Yes, he went in to make enquiries himself.

When will he come back ?

I don't believe he will ever come back.

But if Chandra leaves us, then life is not worth living.

What shall we say to our Leader ?

The Leader also will leave us.

Didn't he leave any message for us before he disappeared ?

Minstrel

He said, "Wait for me. I shall return."

Return ? How are we to know it ?

Minstrel

He said, "I will conquer, and then come back again."

Then we shall wait for him all night.

But, Minstrel, where have we got to wait for him ?

Minstrel

Before that cave, from whence the stream of water comes flowing out.

Which way did he go to get there ?

The darkness there is like a dark sword.

Minstrel

He followed the sound of the night-bird's wings.

Why did you not go with him ?

Minstrel

He left me behind to give you hope.

When did he go ?

Minstrel

In the first hour of the watch.

Now the third hour has passed, I think. The air is chilly.

I dreamt that three women, with their hair hanging loose——

Oh, leave off your dream-women. I am sick of your dreams.

Everything appears darkly ominous. I didn't notice before the hooting of the owl. But now——

Do you hear that dog whining on the far bank of the river?

It seems as though a witch were riding upon him and lashing him.

Surely, if it had been possible, Chandra would have come back by now.

How I wish this night were over.

Do you hear the woman's cry?

Oh, the women, the women. They are ever crying and weeping. But they cannot turn those back, who must go forward.

It is getting unbearable to sit still like this. Men imagine all sorts of things when they sit still. Let us go also. As soon as we are started on our way fear will leave us.

But who will show us the way ?

There is the blind Minstrel.

What do you say, Minstrel ? Can you show us the way ?

Minstrel

Yes.

But we can hardly believe you. How can you find out the path by simply singing ?

If Chandra never comes back, you shall.

We never knew that we loved Chandra so intensely. We made light of him all these days.

When we are in the playing mood, we become so intent on the play, that we neglect the playmate.

But, if he once comes back, we shall never neglect him any more.

I am afraid that we have often given him pain.

Yet his love rose above all that. We never knew how beautiful he was, when we could see him every day.

(*They sing.*)

When there was light in my world
You stood outside my eyes.
Now that there is none,
You come into my heart.
When there were dolls for me, I played;
You smiled and watched from the door.
Now that the dolls have crumbled to dust,
You come and sit by me.
And I have only my heart for my music,
When my lute-strings have broken.

That Minstrel sits so still and silent. I don't like it.

He looks ominous,—like the lowering autumn cloud.

Let us dismiss him.

No, no. It gives us heart, when he sits there.

Don't you see that there is no sign of fear in his face?

It seems as if some messages were striking his forehead. His body appears to espy some one in the distance. There seem to be eyes on the tips of his fingers.

Simply by watching him, we can see that some one is coming through the dark.

Look. He is standing up. He is turning towards the East, and making his obeisance.

Yet there is nothing to be seen, not even a streak of light.

Why not ask him what it is that he sees ?

No, don't disturb him.

Do you know, it seems to me that the morning has dawned in him.

As if the ferry-boat of light had reached the shore of his forehead.

His mind is still, like the morning sky.

The storm of birds' songs will burst out presently.

He is striking his lute. His heart is singing.

Hush. He is singing.

(*The Minstrel sings.*)

Victory to thee, victory for ever,
O brave heart.
Victory to life, to joy, to love,
To eternal light.

The night shall wane, the darkness shall vanish,
Have faith, brave heart.
Wake up from sleep, from languor of despair,
Receive the light of new dawn with a song.

(*A ray of light hovers before the cavern.*)

Ah! There he is. Chandra! Chandra!

Hush. Don't make any noise. I cannot see him distinctly.

Ah! It cannot be any other than Chandra.

Oh, what joy!

Chandra! Come!

Chandra! How could you leave us for so long?

Have you been able to capture the Old Man ?

Chandra

Yes, I have.

But we don't see him.

Chandra

He is coming.

But what did you see in the cave ? Tell us.

Chandra

No, I cannot tell you.

Why ?

Chandra

If my mind were a voice, then I could tell you.

But could you see him, whom you captured ? Was he the Old Man of the World ?

The Old Man who would like to drink up the sea of youth in his insatiable thirst.

Was it the One who is like the dark night, whose eyes are fixed on his breast, whose feet are turned the wrong way round, who walks backwards?

Was it the One who wears the garland of skulls, and lives in the burning-ground of the dead?

Chandra

I do not know, I cannot say. But he is coming. You shall see him.

Minstrel

Yes, I see him.

[*The light strengthens and gradually throughout the scene grows to a culminating brilliance at the close.*]

Where?

Minstrel

Here.

He is coming out of the cave.—
Some one is coming out of the cave.

How wonderful.

Chandra

Why, it is you!

Our Leader!

Our Leader!

Our Leader!

Where is the Old Man?

Leader

He is nowhere.

Nowhere?

Leader

Yes, nowhere.

Then what is he?

Leader

He is a dream.

Then you are the real?

Leader

Yes.

And we are the real?

Leader

Yes.

Those who saw you from behind imagined you in all kinds of shapes.

We didn't recognize you through the dust.

You seemed old.

And then you came out of the cave,—and now you look like a boy.

It seems just as if we had seen you for the first time.

Chandra

You are first every time. You are first over and over again.

Leader

Chandra! You must own your

defeat. You couldn't catch the Old Man.

Chandra

Let our festival begin. The sun is up.

Minstrel, if you keep so still, you will swoon away. Sing something.

(*The Minstrel sings.*)

I lose thee, to find thee back again
and again,
My beloved.
Thou leavest me, that I may receive
thee all the more,
when thou returnest.
Thou canst vanish behind the moment's
screen
Only because thou art mine for ever-
more,
My beloved.
When I go in search of thee, my heart
trembles,
spreading ripples across my love.

Thou smilest through thy disguise of utter absence,
and my tears sweeten thy smile.

Do you hear the hum?

Yes.

They are not bees, but the people of the place.

Then Dada must be near at hand with his quatrains.

Dada

Is this the Leader?

Yes, Dada.

Dada

Oh, I am so glad you have come. I must read my collection of quatrains.

No. No. Not the whole collection, but only one.

Dada

Very well. One will do.

The sun is at the gate of the East,
his drum of victory sounding in
the sky.
The Night says I am blessed, my death
is bliss.
He receives his alms of gold, filling his
wallet,—and departs.

That is to say——

No. We don't want your that is to say.

Dada

It means——

Whatever it means, we are determined not to know it.

Dada

What makes you so desperate ?

It is our festival day.

Dada

Ah ! Is that so ? Then let me go to all the neighbours——

No, you mustn't go there.

Dada

But is there any need for me here?

Yes.

Then my quatrains——

Chandra

We shall colour your quatrains with such a thick brush, that no one will know whether they have any meaning at all.

And then you will be without any means.

The neighbourhood will desert you.

The Watchman will take you to be a fool.

And the Pundit will take you to be a blockhead.

And your own people will consider you to be useless.

And the outside people will consider you queer.

Chandra

But we shall crown you, Dada, with a crown of new leaves.

We shall put a garland of jasmine round your neck.

And there will be no one else except ourselves who will know your true worth.

The Song of the Festival of Spring

[*In which all the persons of the drama, not excepting Sruti-bhushan, unite on the main stage in the dance of Spring.*]

Come and rejoice,
for April is awake.

Fling yourselves into the flood of being,
bursting the bondage of the past.

April is awake.
Life's shoreless sea
is heaving in the sun before you.
All the losses are lost,
and death is drowned in its waves.
Plunge into the deep without fear,
with the gladness of April in your heart.

THE END